The subject matter and vocabulary have been selected with expert assistance, and the brief and simple text is printed in large, clear type.

Children's questions are anticipated and facts presented in a logical sequence. Where possible, the books show what happened in the past and what is relevant today.

Special artwork has been commissioned to set a standard rarely seen in books for this reading age and at this price.

Full-colour illustrations are on all 48 pages to give maximum impact and provide the

t that is the

ird Leaders.

A Ladybird Leader

man
and his car

written by James Webster

illustrated by Gerald Witcomb and Martin Aitchison

Ladybird Books Loughborough

Before the motor car

Once people travelled on horseback
or in coaches pulled by horses.

There was no need to travel very far
or very often.

The picture changes

Now, life has changed.
So many people have motor cars.
Cars seem to be everywhere.

Travel without horses

This was the very first 'car'.
It was driven by steam.
It had three wheels.

Later, cars had petrol engines.
They had solid rubber tyres.
A man had to walk in front
with a red flag to give warning.

Some fine old cars

Some people collect cars like these.
They put them on show.
You can sometimes see them
on the roads.

1907
ROLLS-ROYCE SILVER GHOST

Their owners take great care
of them.

These cars are worth
a lot of money.

The Model T Ford

This is a very old Ford car.
It looked like a box on wheels,
but it worked very well.

This modern car is long and low.
It can go much faster.
It has many more parts.

Making cars

Thousands of people
work in car factories.
The men work on the cars
as they slowly move by.

Few cars . . . many trains

Years ago, most long journeys
were made by railway.
There were many trains.

Many cars . . . fewer trains

More and more people
now use cars.

Roads are more crowded.

There are fewer trains.

Cars and traffic jams

People go to work by car.
They go on holiday by car.

Traffic jams get worse.
They waste time and fuel.
They fill the air with fumes.

Cars fill our streets.
Big car parks have to be made.
Often they are ugly.

Cars take up space at home

More and more houses have a garage.

There is less room for the house.

There is less space to live in.

The extra car

Some families have two cars.
Mothers use one for shopping,
or taking children to school.
All this adds to the traffic.

Cars and fitness

Some people ride in cars
when they could walk.

This man might be fitter
if he walked more.

Seeing places by car

With cars, people can see
more of the country.
They can go to beautiful places.

Too many cars can spoil
these places.

Cars and litter

Litter is ugly.
It can harm animals and birds.
It should be put in litter-bins.

Fire

Too many fires start like this.

We must always be very careful
with fires.

Engine fumes

Engine fumes can spoil
the air we breathe.

Too often we can see and
smell these fumes.

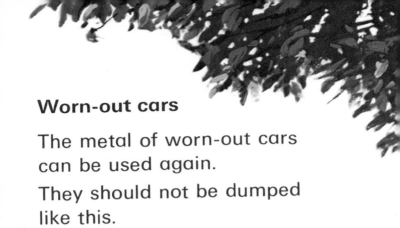

Worn-out cars

The metal of worn-out cars can be used again.

They should not be dumped like this.

Cars can change people

Some people are very polite —

until they drive a car !

Long and heavy loads

More and more heavy loads
are on the roads.
They can hold up other traffic.
Passing them can be dangerous.

In old towns, where streets are narrow, buildings are sometimes damaged.

Cars can break down

Cars must be looked after.
If not, they may break down.

Car repairs

Some car parts wear out.
New ones must be fitted.

Cars can crash

Many people die in crashes
or are hurt in their cars.
Good drivers do not take risks.
They drive carefully.
Their cars have good brakes and tyres

Cars that save lives

This French ambulance
is taking someone to hospital.

Getting there quickly
could save a life.

Away from the road

This car does not need roads.
It can go almost anywhere.
Its engine drives all four wheels.

Soldiers can cross rivers
in this special truck.

Cars for fighting

These armoured cars are going into battle.

They are much faster than tanks.

Towing by car

Cars can tow caravans.
Cars can tow boats.

This car has towed a glider
into the air.

Cars and crime

Some thieves steal cars.
They may use them in robberies.

Police need fast cars
to catch thieves.

Racing cars

These are racing cars.
They have big engines
and very wide tyres.

A very fast car

This car went faster
than any other.
It had a rocket engine.

Its speed was more than
630 miles (1 014 km) an hour.

Some modern cars

Mercedes Benz 450

GW 2

Renault 15

GW 5

Rolls Royce

GW 1

Fiat 500

Mini 1275 G.T.

Maserati Bora

Plymouth
Duster 340

The future of cars

Petrol is made from oil.

Most oil comes from deep wells.

These will not give us oil for ever.

There is not enough oil for everyone.

To save oil, cars in the future
may be driven by electric batteries.
Electric cars could look like this.

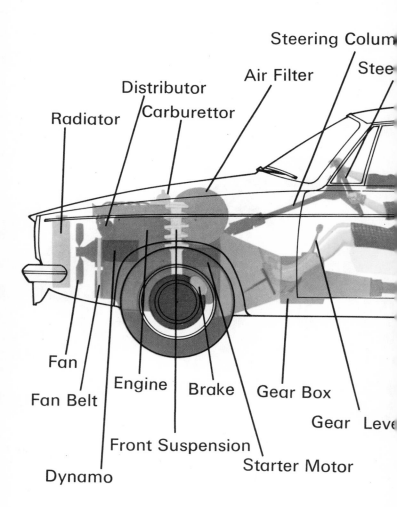

Steering Column

Stee

Air Filter

Distributor

Carburettor

Radiator

Fan

Fan Belt

Engine

Brake

Gear Box

Gear Leve

Front Suspension

Starter Motor

Dynamo

The main par